FREDERICK COUNTY

W9-AOZ-802

EXTREME SUMMER
SPORTS ZONE

MOTO X FREESTYLE

Patrick G. Cain

Lerner Publications Company • Minneapolis

Copyright © 2013 by Lerner Publishing Group, Inc.

All rights reserved. International copyright secured. No part of this book may be reproduced, stored in a retrieval system, or transmitted in any form or by any means—electronic, mechanical, photocopying, recording, or otherwise—without the prior written permission of Lerner Publishing Group, Inc., except for the inclusion of brief quotations in an acknowledged review.

Lerner Publications Company
A division of Lerner Publishing Group, Inc.
241 First Avenue North
Minneapolis, MN 55401 U.S.A.

Website address: www.lernerbooks.com

Content Consultant: Jason Weigandt, senior editor, *Racer X Illustrated*

Library of Congress Cataloging-in-Publication Data

Cain, Patrick G.
    Moto x freestyle / by Patrick G. Cain.
      p. cm. — (Extreme summer sports zone)
    Includes index.
    ISBN 978–1–4677–0753–4 (lib. bdg. : alk. paper)
    1. Motocross—Juvenile literature. I. Title.
GV1060.12.C33 2013
796.7'56—dc23   2012033889

Manufactured in the United States of America
1 – BP – 12/31/12

Photo credits: The images in this book are used with the permission of: Backgrounds: © Henny Ray Abrams/AP Images, 5; © Chris Polk/AP Images, 6; © TOSP Photo/Shutterstock Images, 7; © Raymond Kleboe and Charles Hewitt/Picture Post/Hulton Archive/Getty Images, 8; © AP Images, 9, 10; © David Tucker/Daytona Beach News-Journal/AP Images, 11; © Steve Bruhn/Getty Images, 12; © Mark Sullivan/Wirelmage/Getty Images, 13; © Christian Petersen/Getty Images, 15; © Ovidiu Sopa/Shutterstock Images, 16; © Denis Poroy/AP Images, 17, 24-25; © Shutterstock Images, 18, 19, 22, 28, 29; © iStockphoto, 20; © Diego Barbieri/Shutterstock Images, 21; © Margo Harrison/ Shutterstock Images, 23; © Grant Hindsley/AP Images, 25; © Gautam Singh/AP Images, 26; © Jeff Gross/Getty Images, 27

Front cover: © Dean Treml/AFP/Getty Images (main); © RTimages/Shutterstock.com (background).

Main body text set in Folio Std Light 11/17.
Typeface provided by Adobe Systems.

TABLE OF CONTENTS

CHAPTER ONE
WHAT IS MOTO X FREESTYLE? 4

CHAPTER TWO
MOTOCROSS BEGINS 8

CHAPTER THREE
FREESTYLE BRANDS, EQUIPMENT, AND MOVES 14

CHAPTER FOUR
GOING PRO 24

Glossary 30

For More Information 31

Index 32

About the Author 32

WHAT IS MOTO X FREESTYLE?

Freestyle motocross (moto X) rider Travis Pastrana was an awesome young rider. He won the world freestyle championship in 1998. Before that he had spent years riding and practicing new tricks. All that experience had led to 18 broken bones. Not many athletes continue competing after so many injuries. But Travis always got back on his bike. He was also a good student. He graduated from high school three years early. In 1999 he enrolled at the University of Maryland. Still only a handful of people knew about Travis. But his stardom was about to change. In 1999 ESPN invited the 15-year-old rider to the X Games.

THE X GAMES

ESPN has held an action sports competition called the X Games since 1995. But freestyle motocross wasn't added as an event until 1999. Many fans consider the X Games to be the most important extreme sports competition of the year. Like the Olympic Games, X Games riders compete for gold, silver, or bronze medals. X Games winners also get prize money. Pro riders usually work for months on trying to perfect their routines or specific moves.

Stars like Travis Pastrana have helped make freestyle motocross one of the most popular action sports.

Travis Pastrana celebrates after winning the 2003 X Games moto X freestyle competition.

In 1999 freestyle motocross was still young. Few people knew what was possible on dirt bikes. Motocross racers had been racing off-road motorcycles for years. But these races were all about speed. In freestyle motocross, riders used a series of jumps to do daring tricks. In fact, the 1999 X Games were the first to include freestyle motocross. The sport hadn't come into the national spotlight yet. It needed attention. It needed eye-popping moments. It needed stars.

Travis gave the sport what it needed. He revved up his bike for the 1999 X Games. In 90 seconds, Travis changed the way motocross riders would compete for years to come. He sent his Suzuki bike soaring into the sky. He pushed the limits. He invented tricks. He jumped nearly 30 feet (9 meters) high. And he scored a 99 out of 100 to win the gold medal. Nobody has been able to beat that freestyle score. The 15-year-old kid became an action sports legend.

The win was great for Travis. It was also a big day for freestyle motocross. Travis would win many more gold medals at the X Games. The young freestyle rider had changed his sport forever. Freestyle motocross is still one of the most popular X Games sports. It is an exciting time to be a freestyle rider!

Freestyle motocross has gotten even more popular since the late 1990s. Freestyle riders still show off amazing tricks.

CHAPTER TWO

MOTOCROSS BEGINS

Motocross riding has changed a lot over the course of its history. But it was a popular event long before freestyle riders came on the scene. Early riders perfected their skills in other motocross events. For the first few decades of the sport, Europe was the home of motocross. In the early 1900s, riders competed in off-road motorcycle trials in the United Kingdom. Then, in 1924, riders competed in an English off-road event called Scrambles. Back then motocross bikes were bicycles with small engines. Riders raced on a 50-mile (80-kilometer) course. These courses were usually rugged with steep hills. Every course was different. Soon the event became popular in France. The French added small jumps to their courses.

Scrambling took place on rough, dirt courses with hills.

In the 1970s riders began catching air on supercross courses.

U.S. Motocross

By the mid-1960s, motocross came to the United States. And the sport was changing. Early American motocross still didn't feature huge jumps. American riders participated in an event known as supercross. Supercross brought the sport into indoor stadiums. Supercross riders raced around a track with jumps and obstacles. These challenges made the race about both speed and skill. The sport became more consistent. The indoor tracks could be copied. Spectators could watch the sport more easily. From the very first supercross competition in 1972 in Los Angeles, California, riders wanted to catch more air (jump higher).

Bikes were changing too. Bike makers were improving suspension systems (the system of springs that absorbs shock when landing). Riders could land bigger tricks. Other improvements meant bikes could take sharper turns.

Evel Knievel wowed huge crowds with his daring motorcycle stunts.

In the 1960s and the 1970s, the world also had its first freestyle-like superstar. Evel Knievel was a famous stuntman. He didn't race. He was a daredevil. He made huge jumps on his motorcycle. He shocked the world with his daring tricks. Knievel helped make freestyle motocross popular.

Throughout the 1970s and the 1980s, motocross racing events became even more popular. Jumps kept getting bigger. Bikes kept getting faster. But jumps were still not launching points for tricks. When a rider raced and took a jump, the point of the jump was to land as soon and as safely as possible. The event was a race. The riders did not have much time to try big tricks. But all that would change.

The Rise of Freestyle Motocross

In the 1990s, rider Jeremy McGrath was known as the king of supercross. He won race after race. He shattered records. During one race, he did something no one had ever seen before. He kicked his leg back behind him when coming off the jump. He called the trick a nac-nac. Many riders consider this trick to be the birth of freestyle motocross. Riders still perform nac-nacs in competitions.

Jeremy McGrath was a supercross rider who helped pioneer freestyle motocross.

Supercross rider James "Bubba" Stewart shows off a nac-nac. He is famous for being the first African American athlete to have success as a pro motocross rider.

Other racers began innovating new tricks to match McGrath's nac-nac, even though they were competing as racers. Finally, in the late 1990s, small, judged freestyle events started popping up. Travis Pastrana won the first world freestyle championship in 1998. In 1999 ESPN added a freestyle event to its summer X Games. Travis Pastrana won his first gold medal. Mike Cinqmars took silver.

That same year, another extreme sports event known as the Gravity Games held its first freestyle motocross event. Again, Pastrana took gold. Rider Ronnie Faisst took silver. At the 2003 Gravity Games, pro Nate Adams became the first rider to beat Pastrana in a competition. Riders kept getting better, and tricks kept getting bigger. New stars such as Taka Higashino kept pushing the limits of the sport. Freestyle motocross was around to stay.

NATE ADAMS

Like many pros, Nate Adams started riding at a young age. He was only eight years old when he took up motocross. He went pro at the age of 17. Not long after going pro, Adams won the 2002 World Freestyle Motocross Championship. He became a legend in 2003 when he was the first rider to beat Travis Pastrana in a freestyle competition. Adams won X Games gold medals in freestyle in 2004 and 2011. He took fourth place in freestyle at the 2012 X Games.

Nate Adams has helped push the limits of freestyle motocross since the sport's early days.

CHAPTER THREE

FREESTYLE BRANDS, EQUIPMENT, AND MOVES

A pro freestyler can't ride without the right equipment. Brands are very important to freestyle motocross. Motocross brands represent bikes, beverages, and clothing. For an amateur rider, getting sponsored by one of these brands can be a huge step toward going pro. These brands also sponsor many freestyle competitions.

Getting Sponsored

Freestyle motocross is a risky sport. A rider needs to spend a lot of time practicing a trick to perform it safely. Riders may not have time to practice if they need another job to earn money. Pro riders have sponsors who support them financially. With the help of a sponsor, freestyle motocross can be a pro's full-time job.

RONNIE FAISST

Ronnie Faisst rode a motorcycle for the first time at the age of eight. The rest was history. He went pro as a supercross rider when he was 18 years old. Two years later, he moved to California, where he met freestyler riders Brian Deegan and Carey Hart. By 1999 Faisst was a sponsored freestyle rider. He earned a silver medal at the 1999 Gravity Games that year. But he didn't stop there. He continued riding and competing in different motocross events. In 2011 and 2012 he earned bronze medals in the X Games motocross speed and style competition.

Ronnie Faisst competes at the 2005 X Games moto x freestyle event.

Once a rider becomes a professional, he or she may get invited to events. The rider will be paid to show up and ride. If a rider wins the event, that pro will get paid even more. Companies such as Red Bull, Rockstar Energy Drink, and Monster Energy Drink are major sponsors of freestyle motocross teams and riders. When a rider does an awesome trick, the sponsoring company gets great advertising. Some riders also make money by appearing in commercials or other advertisements for a brand they represent.

Pros will often create their own brands and teams to sponsor riders. Riders Brian Deegan and Larry Linkogle started a clothing line called Metal Mulisha. The brand makes clothes in the casual style freestylers love. Metal Mulisha is also one of the most well-known freestyle motocross sponsors. Metal Mulisha still sponsors some of the best freestyle riders, including Ronnie Faisst and Todd Potter.

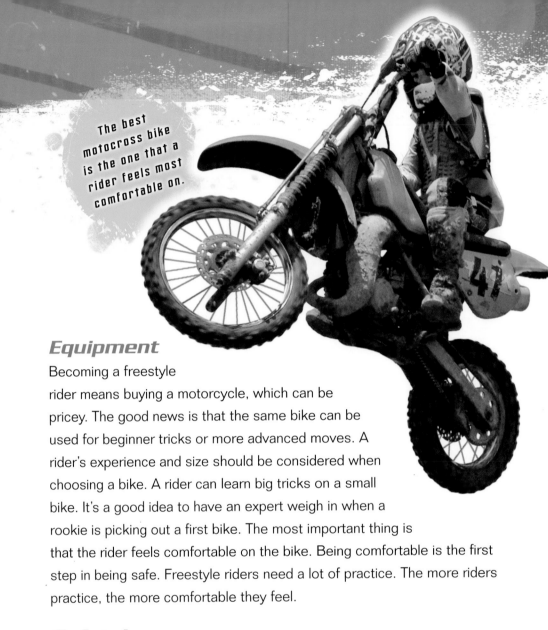

The best motocross bike is the one that a rider feels most comfortable on.

Equipment

Becoming a freestyle rider means buying a motorcycle, which can be pricey. The good news is that the same bike can be used for beginner tricks or more advanced moves. A rider's experience and size should be considered when choosing a bike. A rider can learn big tricks on a small bike. It's a good idea to have an expert weigh in when a rookie is picking out a first bike. The most important thing is that the rider feels comfortable on the bike. Being comfortable is the first step in being safe. Freestyle riders need a lot of practice. The more riders practice, the more comfortable they feel.

Safety!

All action sports can be dangerous. But freestyle motocross involves some of the greatest risks. A rookie rider can stay safe by riding within his or her skill level. Riders can be seriously injured trying big tricks before they are ready. Riders take practice runs into a foam pit. The soft landing reduces the risk of injuries.

Experienced freestyle riders try for huge tricks. But these tricks aren't always easy to land. Crashes are part of the sport. Even pro riders take falls during practice and competitions. If a pro is injured, that rider may not be able to compete. An injured rider may not get paid. Because of these risks, pro riders recommend some must-have safety gear.

To stay safe, freestyle rider Todd Potter practices new tricks by jumping into a foam pit.

FREESTYLE SAFETY GEAR

BOOTS

Motocross boots are made with plastic or even steel. They are designed to help protect a rider's feet, ankles, and shins while doing tricks and while crashing.

HELMET

Even pros crash when they are learning new tricks. A helmet helps keep a crash from seriously injuring a rider. Helmets are required in the X Games moto x freestyle competition. Most motocross helmets feature colorful graphic designs.

GLOVES

Gloves protect a rider's hands from getting cut up on the dirt and gravel of the freestyle course. Gloves also help a freestyle rider keep a solid grip on his or her bike while going off jumps.

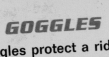

GOGGLES

Goggles protect a rider's eyes from the dust and sand that the bike kicks up on the dirt freestyle course. Goggles are especially important to help a rider see while landing jumps.

NECK BRACE

If riders injure their necks in a fall, they may be paralyzed for life or even die. Because of this danger, many pros choose to ride with a neck brace.

KNEE AND ELBOW GUARDS

Many riders also choose to wear knee guards and elbow guards. Knee guards act as braces that keep knees from twisting on hard landings. Elbow guards protect a rider's elbows while landing or crashing.

19

A no-footer is the next step for a rookie rider who can handle small jumps.

The Moves

Rookie riders need to spend a lot of time on a bike before trying tricks. A rider must learn where the bike's pegs and handlebars are. A rider needs to learn how to change gears on the bike. Once a new rider feels comfortable, it may be time to try very small jumps. Landing little jumps helps a rider's body get used to the impact. A rider should try to land the bike in the same position every time. Once riders have mastered small jumps, they can start trying bigger tricks. A rider can practice taking one foot off the pegs while in the air. Eventually, the rider might try removing both feet. This move is called a no-footer. Then the rider may try taking his or her hands off the handlebars. Learning tricks takes time. Eventually riders can try combining tricks to create moves known as combos.

Here are some tricks fans might see the pros pulling off at freestyle competitions:

Grab

To do a grab, the rider hangs on to the seat or back of the bike while airborne. Freestyle motocross riders do many different types of grabs. In a double grab, the rider grabs the seat while kicking his or her legs off the back of the bike. Pros often use grabs in combos with other tricks.

Can Can

In a can can, the rider takes one foot off the peg after going off a jump. Then the rider brings the foot to the other side of the bike while airborne. Both legs are on one side of the bike while in midair.

A double grab is an important trick for a pro freestyle rider.

Pros do backflips in many motocross freestyle competitions.

Backflip

A backflip is one of the toughest tricks a freestyler can do. Pros often combine backflips with grabs or other tricks for a higher score.

Superman

To do a superman trick, riders keep their hands on the handlebars while kicking their feet off the back of the bike. When the trick is done right, riders look as though they are flying.

MOTO X BEST TRICK

In 2001 the X Games added a freestyle competition for riders dedicated to catching the biggest air. The competition was known as big air, but the name was later changed to best trick. In best trick, a rider uses a ramp to do a huge trick that will wow judges. Unlike moto X freestyle, the event is not timed. Riders get two chances to perform an awesome move. Because freestyle and best trick are so similar, many freestyle riders also compete in the best trick competition.

Cliffhanger

In a cliffhanger, the pro stands straight up on the bike while airborne. The rider moves up the bike until the handlebars are resting on the rider's toes. Then the pro throws his or her hands up in the air as if on a roller coaster.

The cliffhanger trick is one of the toughest freestyle tricks.

GOING PRO

Skateboarders or BMX bikers can practice just about anywhere there is pavement. Freestyle motocross riders are not so lucky. Freestyle motocross takes a lot of space, so it is nearly impossible to train in a city. Riders need a course with practice jumps, which means a lot of dirt. Most young riders learn with the help of an experienced rider with access to a freestyle training course. Metal Mulisha has a compound with freestyle courses and foam pits. The team may invite a talented young rider to practice at the compound.

Rockstar Energy Drink helps support rider Javier Villegas. Villegas won the bronze medal at the 2012 X Games moto x freestyle event.

Todd Potter practices at the Metal Mulisha Compound.

Most freestyle riders never have the chance to ride at a professional level. They ride because they love the sport. But with enough practice, a rider may get the chance to compete in an amateur competition. At amateur events, a company or a team may notice a skilled rider. When a team or a company offers to sponsor the rider, the rider can compete professionally.

The Crusty Demons are a professional motocross team whose members practice together.

Team Riding

Most pros ride on teams. Major companies such as Red Bull or Monster often sponsor these teams. But freestyle motocross teams are very different from those of other sports such as baseball. Motocross teammates don't win and lose together. Each team member is an independent rider. Teammates even compete against one another at events.

The Events

Pro freestyle riders come together for many major events throughout the year. Red Bull sponsors several competitions. Monster sponsors freestyle motocross events around the world. But for most freestyle fans, the biggest event is ESPN's X Games. Japanese rider Taka Higashino is one of the best freestyle riders. In 2012 he dominated the X Games with a score of 93.33 to win the gold medal. His winning run included a brand-new trick—the backflip Rock Solid double grab.

Taka Higashino celebrates his gold medal after winning the moto x freestyle event at the 2012 X Games.

TAKA HIGASHINO

Taka Higashino was the 2012 X Games freestyle motocross champion. He is also the first Japanese motocross competitor to medal at the X Games. His 2012 runs were not his first time impressing the judges. In 2010 he took bronze in the best trick competition. He came close again in 2011. That year he took fourth place in both freestyle and best trick.

WOMEN IN FREESTYLE

Women's motocross racing has been a popular X Games event for many years. Other female racing events take place around the world. However, women's freestyle motocross has not caught on in the same way that women's racing has. In 2012 the X Games still had not introduced a women's class in the freestyle competition. But a few women ride freestyle and are trying to increase interest in the sport. In 2002 female freestyle riders rode in an exhibition event at the X Games. The event showed the world what women could do on their bikes. Heather Williams and Heidi Henry are two female freestylers who are working hard to make the sport mainstream.

Judging

In a freestyle motocross competition, riders have a set amount of time to do tricks on a dirt course. In most events, riders have 60 seconds. The course features jumps, ramps, and other obstacles. Most riders attempt six to eight moves in a run. Judges rate the run on a scale of 1 to 100. Judges consider the difficulty of the tricks as well as how well the rider preforms the tricks. The more a run impresses the judges, the higher the score. Each rider gets two runs. The highest score is the rider's final score. The highest freestyle X Games score is still Travis Pastrana's 99 from 1999.

Women's freestyle motocross events are still very uncommon, but women's motocross racing is a popular sport with a huge following.

Freestyle motocross is an exciting sport with big tricks and big air. But freestyle riders need to stay safe while riding.

Where to Watch

ESPN's X Games is shown on national cable television and the ABC network. Fans can rewatch clips from the X Games online year-round. Many riders also film themselves doing awesome tricks. Freestyle highlights from pros and amateurs alike are available every day through video-sharing websites such as YouTube. Fans who don't want to wait for the X Games can have a parent or adult help find videos online. But beginning riders need to be careful. Trying to copy the moves shown online can lead to an injury.

GLOSSARY

AMATEUR
someone who participates in an activity for fun without expectation of payment

COMBOS
groups of tricks done together

DAREDEVIL
someone who enjoys risky activities

EXHIBITION
a public showing of a noncompetitive event

MAINSTREAM
something that is commonly accepted

PROFESSIONAL
someone who participates in an activity as a job for payment

ROOKIE
someone who is new to a sport or activity

SPONSOR
a company that financially supports professional athletes in a sport so they can focus on that sport

SUSPENSION SYSTEM
a system of springs that absorbs shock on a motocross bike

FOR MORE INFORMATION

Further Reading

Cain, Patrick G. *Moto X Best Trick*. Minneapolis: Lerner Publications, 2013.

Levy, Jane. *Freestyle Motocross*. New York: Rosen, 2007.

Savage, Jeff. *Travis Pastrana*. Minneapolis, Lerner Publications, 2006.

Zuehlke, Jeffrey. *Motorcycle Road Racing*. Minneapolis: Lerner Publications, 2009.

Websites

ESPN X Games
http://espn.go.com/action/xgames
The official X Games website features information about the X Games. Check out freestyle motocross athlete bios, videos, and scores, and find out when and where the next X Games will be held.

Heidi Henry Talks Motocross
http://www.kidzworld.com/article/3379-heidi-henry-talks-motocross#
Learn more about the exciting sport of freestyle motocross from freestyle rider Heidi Henry.

What Is Freestyle Motocross
http://www.livestrong.com/article/243446-what-is-freestyle-motocross/
Check out this website to learn more about freestyle motocross. The site features information on the sport's history, safety tips, and motocross bikes.

INDEX

Adams, Nate, 12, 13

backflips, 22, 27
brands, 14–15

can cans, 21
Cinqmars, Mike, 12
cliffhangers, 23
combos, 20, 21
competitions, 4, 9, 11, 12, 13, 14, 17, 18, 21, 25, 26–29

Deegan, Brian, 14, 15

ESPN, 4, 12, 27, 29

Faisst, Ronnie, 12, 14, 15
foam pits, 16, 24
freestyle motocross courses, 8, 18, 19, 24, 28
freestyle motocross moves, 4, 16, 20–23, 28
freestyle motocross safety, 16–19
freestyle motocross teams, 15, 24, 26

grabs, 21, 22, 27
Gravity Games, 12, 14

Hart, Carey, 14
Henry, Heidi, 28
Higashino, Taka, 12, 27

jumps, 6, 7, 8, 9, 10–11, 18, 19, 20, 21, 24, 28

Knievel, Evel, 10

Linkogle, Larry, 15

McGrath, Jeremy, 11–12
Metal Mulisha, 15, 24
Monster Energy Drink, 15, 26, 27
motocross bikes, 4, 6, 7, 8, 9, 11, 14, 16, 18, 19, 20–23, 28
motocross history, 4–7, 8–12
moto X best trick, 22, 27
moto X freestyle scoring, 7, 22, 27, 28

nac-nacs, 11–12
no-footers, 20

Pastrana, Travis, 4–7, 12, 13, 28
Potter, Todd, 15

Red Bull, 15, 26, 27

safety gear, 17, 18–19
Scrambles, 8
sponsors, 14–15, 25, 26, 27
supercross, 9, 11, 14
superman tricks, 22

videos, 29

Williams, Heather, 28
women's freestyle motocross, 28
World Freestyle Motocross Championships, 4, 12, 13

X Games, 4, 6, 7, 12, 13, 14, 18, 22, 27–29

About the Author

Patrick Cain is a nuclear engineer turned writer. He is an award-winning journalist whose work often appears in a number of magazines such as *ESPN the Magazine*, and *Fast Company*. He currently lives in Los Angeles, California, but will forever be tied to upstate New York.

MAR   2015   2 1982 02829 3029